Using Earth's Underground Heat

by Nancy White

Consultant: Frank Robbins, LEED AP
(Leadership in Energy and Environmental Design,
Accredited Professional)

BEARPORT
PUBLISHING

New York, New York

Credits

Cover and Title Page, © Clarence Holmes/Shutterstock; 6–7, © Yann Arthus-Bertrand/Corbis; 8, © E.J. Baumeister Jr./Alamy; 10–11, © Geo-Heat Center/DOE/National Renewable Energy Laboratory (NREL); 12, © Ann S. Lundy/DOE/National Renewable Energy Laboratory (NREL); 14–15, © Bruce Green/DOE/National Renewable Energy Laboratory (NREL); 16, © Warren Gretz/DOE/National Renewable Energy Laboratory (NREL); 17, © Warren Gretz/DOE/National Renewable Energy Laboratory (NREL); 18–19, © Baloncici/Shutterstock; 20–21, Courtesy of Department of Energy; 22–23, © Hannamariah/Shutterstock; 24, © Gimmi Gimmi/Photolibrary; 25, © Sue Ashe/Shutterstock; 26L, © Frank Kovalchek; 26R, © 2009 Patrick Endres/AlaskaStock.com; 28, © Porterfield-Chickering/Photo Researchers, Inc.; 30, © Pixtal/SuperStock.

Publisher: Kenn Goin
Editorial Director: Adam Siegel
Creative Director: Spencer Brinker
Photo Researcher: Amy Dunleavy

The Going Green series is printed on recycled paper.

Library of Congress Cataloging-in-Publication Data

White, Nancy.
  Using earth's underground heat / by Nancy White.
     p. cm. — (Going green)
  Includes bibliographical references and index.
  ISBN-13: 978-1-59716-963-9 (library binding)
  ISBN-10: 1-59716-963-3 (library binding)
  1. Geothermal resources—Juvenile literature. I. Title.

GB1199.5.W47 2010
333.8'8—dc22
                        2009015119

For more information, write to Bearport Publishing Company, Inc., 101 Fifth Avenue, Suite 6R, New York, New York 10003. Printed in the United States of America.

10 9 8 7 6 5 4 3 2 1

Contents

The Heat Beneath Our Feet

Every day we use heat for cooking and washing. We heat air inside buildings to keep us warm. We even use heat to make electricity. Where does this heat come from? Most of it comes from burning **fossil fuels**—coal, oil, and gas. Some of it, however, comes from deep inside Earth.

Earth's **core**, or center, is thought to be hotter than the surface of the sun. It warms the planet from the inside out. The core's heat also warms water that seeps deep into the ground from rain and melting snow. This **groundwater** can become as hot as 700°F (371°C). For thousands of years, people have been using this hot water, called **geothermal** water, in many ways.

Scientists use the term *geothermal energy* to describe Earth's underground heat. The word *geothermal* comes from the Greek words *geo*, meaning "earth," and *therme*, meaning "heat."

A Look Inside Earth

Earth is made up of four layers—the inner core, the outer core, the mantle, and the crust.

Crust

Mantle

Outer core

Inner core

Earth is hottest at its inner core, where the temperature may reach 12,600°F (6,982°C). The inner core is made mostly of iron.

The outer core is hot melted rock, called magma.

The mantle is made up of rock and magma.

The crust is made up of rocks and soil.

Using Earth's Heat

Where do people find geothermal water? In some places, it comes up through openings in Earth's surface. Sometimes a jet of hot water called a **geyser** shoots out of the ground. Geysers, however, are very rare. More often, steaming hot water bubbles up to the surface in pools called **hot springs**.

Thousands of years ago, people began using water from hot springs for cooking and bathing. Today, people still go to **spas** to relax in the warm springs or in pools filled with geothermal water.

Animals, as well as humans, have been bathing in hot springs for thousands of years. The water helps these Japanese macaques stay warm during the winter.

The water from geysers and hot springs comes up to Earth's surface naturally. Scientists and **engineers**, however, are finding ways to bring up more of this hot, underground water. Why? Geothermal water is used for more than just cooking and bathing. People also use it to heat buildings and make electricity—sometimes without burning fossil fuels!

Hot springs can be found on all continents and in many countries, including Iceland, New Zealand, Japan, and the United States.

The Problem with Fossil Fuels

Why is burning fossil fuels a problem? There are three important reasons.

One reason is that coal, oil, and gas are not **renewable** sources of energy. They cannot be replaced once they are used up, so they will eventually run out.

Another reason is that fossil fuels give off **poisonous** chemicals when they are burned. They **pollute** the air and water, which can kill plants and wildlife.

Fossil fuels are burned at this power plant to make electricity.

About 85 percent of the energy used in the United States comes from burning fossil fuels.

Finally, when fossil fuels are burned they release **greenhouse gases**, such as **carbon dioxide**, which can contribute to **global warming**. How? Greenhouse gases trap heat from the sun in Earth's **atmosphere**. If too many greenhouse gases are released into the atmosphere, the world will get too warm. Plants and animals that are used to cooler temperatures may die.

Unlike fossil fuels, geothermal energy is both **clean** and renewable. It doesn't harm Earth's environment—and it won't run out!

What Causes Global Warming?

sun

2 Some heat coming from the warm Earth goes back into space.

3 Some heat coming from the warm Earth is trapped in the atmosphere by greenhouse gases—creating global warming.

atmosphere

1 The sun's heat warms Earth.

Earth

Heating for a Town

In some areas, the buildings in a town can be heated by using geothermal water. How can this be done? People drill a hole into the earth to reach geothermal water, which is then pumped up through pipes. The town's supply of cold water is carried by separate pipes. Both sets of pipes go through a **heat exchanger** where they pass near each other. The town's cold water **absorbs** the heat from the geothermal water and becomes hot.

Some of this heated water is piped through the walls and floors of homes, schools, and other buildings to warm the inside air. Some of the heated water also becomes the town's hot water supply. After the geothermal water releases its heat, it is pumped back into the ground, where Earth's heat will warm it again.

In Klamath Falls, Oregon, pipes that stretch for one mile (1.6 km) bring geothermal water into the city to heat the town's water supply.

To melt snow and ice, pipes that carry geothermal water are buried under these sidewalks in Klamath Falls, Oregon.

Pumping Up the Heat

Some areas don't have geothermal water underground. In those places, a machine called a geothermal heat pump can use Earth's heat to warm buildings. This is possible because about four feet (1.2 m) under the ground the temperature of the soil is always around 55°F (12.8°C). Earth's inner heat, as well as heat from the sun, keep this temperature steady.

To use a geothermal heat pump, people first dig a hole into the ground about 6 to 12 feet (1.8 to 3.7 m) deep outside a building. Pipes go from the building, into the hole, and back into the building. Then a liquid, such as water or **antifreeze**, is put into the pipes. The pump keeps the liquid flowing in a circle.

As the liquid moves through the pipes, it absorbs heat from the earth. When the warm liquid is carried into the building, it gives off heat that warms the inside air. The liquid continues moving through the pipes, back into the ground, where the earth warms it again.

Geothermal heat pumps keep the temperature inside this school in Lincoln, Nebraska, comfortable all year round.

How a Geothermal Heat Pump Warms a House

Liquid is pumped into the ground and warmed by Earth's heat.

Even in hot weather, the temperature of the ground stays at around 55°F (12.8°C). Therefore, a heat pump can act as an air conditioner. In the summer, the liquid in the underground pipes is cooler than the air in the house so it can absorb the heat as it is pumped through the building. The liquid is then cooled in the ground and pumped back into the house to take in more heat.

Liquid warmed by Earth's heat is pumped into the house.

Heat for Crops

Some buildings are heated to keep people warm. Greenhouses are heated to keep plants warm. With enough heat, farmers can grow flowers and food **crops** inside these buildings all year long.

The glass walls of a greenhouse trap heat from the sun. However, in cold weather even more heat is needed to keep a greenhouse warm enough to grow plants. Fortunately, some greenhouses can be warmed using geothermal water. How does this work?

Pipes that carry geothermal water are placed along a greenhouse's walls and under its soil. The air and soil in the greenhouse become warm as they absorb the water's heat. Flowers and crops such as tomatoes, cucumbers, and lettuce can then be grown in the greenhouse all year.

These flowers were grown in a greenhouse in Idaho that is warmed by geothermal water.

In Iceland, a country that is near the North Pole, geothermal water keeps greenhouses warm enough to grow bananas and pineapples—fruits that are grown mainly in hot, tropical countries.

Fish and Alligator Farms

While geothermal water can help grow plants in greenhouses, it can also help people grow another kind of food—fish. Many of the fish people eat are raised in tanks on **fish farms**. Sometimes, however, these farms are located in places where it is too cold for the fish to live. To solve this problem, some fish farms use a combination of hot geothermal water and cold water to keep the temperature in the fish tanks just right all year.

Fish Breeders of Idaho is a company that uses geothermal water to warm its fish tanks. This farm produces more than 500,000 pounds (226,796 kg) of fish per year!

Geothermal water was used to raise these tilapia on a fish farm in Colorado.

Alligators need warm water to live in. Yet that doesn't stop farmers in Idaho and Colorado from raising them. They simply add geothermal water to the alligator ponds so that they stay warm—even when air temperatures drop below freezing in the winter.

These alligators are being raised on a farm in Colorado that uses geothermal water to keep the animals warm. Alligator hides are used to make boots, wallets, and watch bands, and their meat is becoming a popular food.

Drying Food

Geothermal energy is used in other ways besides heating homes, buildings, and water. It is also used to dry foods. One of the benefits of dried foods is that they last a long time and don't have to be refrigerated.

A **plant** at Brady's Hot Springs, Nevada, dries more than 50 million pounds (22,679,619 kg) of onions each year. Hot air makes the moisture in the onions **evaporate**, or dry up. The air is heated by geothermal water that is piped in from nearby hot springs. The plant sells its dried onions to fast food restaurants.

Some of the fruit people buy in supermarkets is also dried. A lot of this dried fruit—including pineapple, mango, banana, apple, and pear—comes from Central America. The fruit is dried in the same way as the onions in Nevada.

Other foods dried by geothermal heat include fish from Iceland, tomatoes from India, and apricots, prunes, and figs from Greece.

Making Electricity

One of the most important ways that people use geothermal energy is to make electricity. The electricity that people use is produced in **power plants** by machines called **generators**. A generator is powered by the spinning blades of a **turbine**. Steam from boiling water makes the blades spin. In some places, geothermal water is so hot that it gives off steam. While most power plants burn coal to boil water that will create steam, some plants today get their steam from geothermal water.

A geothermal power plant releases less than 1 percent of the carbon-dioxide emissions released by a power plant that burns fossil fuels.

The Geysers is a group of geothermal power plants in northern California that can produce enough electricity to power 725,000 homes, or a city the size of San Francisco.

Is Geothermal the Answer?

Using Earth's underground heat has many benefits. One of the most important of these is that geothermal heat is a renewable source of energy. Another is that it saves users a lot of money. For example, geothermal heat pumps can reduce heating costs by 30 to 70 percent and cooling costs by 20 to 50 percent!

On the other hand, the use of geothermal energy does have a few drawbacks. One of them is that geothermal power plants can be built only where there is hot water underground. Another drawback is that it's expensive to drill for geothermal water.

Even with these drawbacks, however, one thing is certain. People can't keep depending only on fuels that are harmful to the environment and that will eventually be used up. Instead, we will need to use cleaner and more renewable sources for heat and electricity. Geothermal energy is sure to be one of them.

In Reykjavik (RAY-kyuh-VEEK), the capital of Iceland, 95 percent of all homes are heated by geothermal energy.

Reykjavik, Iceland

Geothermal History Highlights

People have been using Earth's underground heat for thousands of years. Here are some highlights in geothermal history:

- **10,000 Years Ago** Native Americans use hot springs for bathing and cooking.

- **2,000 Years Ago** People use hot springs for bathing and washing in ancient Rome.

- **1892** Boise, Idaho, becomes the first city in the United States to use a geothermal heating system.

- **Early 1900s** The world's first geothermal power plant begins operating in Larderello, Italy.

- **1960s** The first large geothermal power plant in the United States, The Geysers, begins operating in northern California.

- **2005** Seventy-two countries around the world use geothermal energy.

The world's first geothermal power plant was built in Larderello, Italy.

So Many Uses

In addition to providing heat for buildings, greenhouses, fish farms, and food-drying plants, geothermal energy is used in many other ways. Here are a few examples:

- **Gold mining** Gold is found in rocks. To get the gold out, the rocks are crushed. Then the crushed rock has to be separated from the gold. Hot water is used in this process. Two gold mines in Nevada use geothermally heated water to help separate the gold from the rock.

- **Dying cloth** Steam or hot water is needed to **dye** cloth. The hot water helps the colored dye stay in the cloth so that it doesn't wash out. Geothermal steam is often used for this purpose.

- **Drying lumber** Freshly cut wood contains sap, a sticky liquid inside trees. If the sap is not removed from the wood, the wood sometimes warps or bends. Therefore, lumber used for making furniture and building homes needs to be dried. It is put into a huge oven called a kiln. At the lumber plant in Kawerau, New Zealand, the kiln for drying lumber uses geothermal heat.

Using Heat to Keep Cool: The Aurora Ice Museum

People come to the Chena Hot Springs Resort near Fairbanks, Alaska, to relax in the natural outdoor hot springs and enjoy the beautiful scenery. Another attraction at the resort is the Aurora Ice Museum.

- Inside the museum, everything is made completely from ice and snow, including beds, chairs, and glasses.

- The museum has rooms where guests can sleep in fur sleeping bags on a bed of ice.

- During the cold winters in Alaska, everything inside the hotel stays frozen at around 20°F (–7°C).

- In the summer, however, temperatures in Fairbanks can go up to 90°F (32°C). The heat could melt everything inside the museum.

- Air-conditioning the museum using electricity produced from burning fossil fuels would be very expensive. So the building is kept cool by a "chiller." This air-conditioning system runs on electricity generated by geothermal heat—which is much cheaper.

How a Geothermal Power Plant Works

Here is how the most common kind of geothermal power plant works to generate electricity:

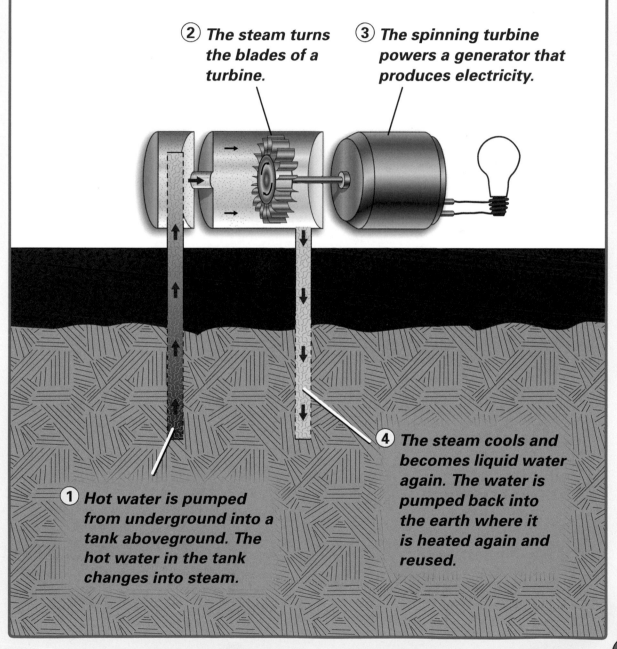

② **The steam turns the blades of a turbine.**

③ **The spinning turbine powers a generator that produces electricity.**

④ **The steam cools and becomes liquid water again. The water is pumped back into the earth where it is heated again and reused.**

① **Hot water is pumped from underground into a tank aboveground. The hot water in the tank changes into steam.**

A Clean City

Reykjavik, the capital of Iceland, was once one of the world's most polluted cities. Now it is considered one of the cleanest. Why?

- Around 95 percent of all the homes in Reykjavik are warmed by geothermal heat.
- Geothermal water is used to heat water for swimming pools, washing machines, and showers.
- Geothermal water is piped under streets to melt ice and snow.
- Fruits and vegetables are grown in greenhouses heated by geothermal water.

The Blue Lagoon is one of the most popular tourist attractions in Reykjavik. This geothermal spa uses the hot water from a nearby geothermal plant to heat its outdoor pool.

Research for the Future

One problem with using geothermal water is that it can be used only where there is a supply of hot groundwater. Yet scientists and engineers are working to solve that problem for the future. They are developing a method called "hot dry rock technology," also referred to as "enhanced geothermal systems" (EGS). How does it work?

- If people dig five to ten miles (8 to 16 km) below Earth's surface, they will hit very hot rock.

- **Wells** can be dug down into the hot rock.

- Cold water that is pumped down into the wells will be heated by the hot rock.

- The heated water can then be pumped back up to Earth's surface where it turns into steam to be used in a geothermal power plant.

- When the steam cools, it becomes liquid water again. The liquid is pumped back down into the rock to be heated again and reused.

Five miles (8 km) is a long way to dig. Yet engineers are studying and researching ways to do it. When they perfect their techniques, clean, renewable geothermal heat may be available to people all over the world.

How Hot Dry Rock Technology Works

Power plant

1 *Cold water is pumped into wells deep below Earth's surface.*

3 *Heated water is pumped back up to Earth's surface where it turns to steam that powers a generator.*

2 *Water is heated by hot rock.*

Hot Rock

29

Most of the heat and electricity that people use comes from burning fossil fuels. Hopefully, in the future, that will no longer be true. For now, however, everyone should try to make his or her "carbon footprint" as small as possible.

What is your carbon footprint? It is the total amount of greenhouse gases a person releases into the atmosphere by burning fossil fuels. Using geothermal energy instead of fossil fuels is one way to shrink a person's carbon footprint. Here are a few other ways:

- Turn off all appliances when they're not being used, incuding TVs and computers. Also, unplug cell-phone chargers.

- If possible, walk or bike instead of asking an adult for a car ride.

- Reduce the amount of hot water you use by taking shorter showers.

- Wear warm clothing inside your home when it's cold outside, so you don't have to turn up the heat so much.

- When it's hot outside, dress lightly, and use fans in your home as often as possible, instead of air conditioners.

Ask an adult to help you e-mail your representatives in Congress. Let them know that you support research to find new ways of using geothermal energy for heating and electricity.

Learn More Online

To learn more about geothermal energy, visit **www.bearportpublishing.com/GoingGreen**

Glossary

absorbs (ab-ZORBZ) to soak up something

antifreeze (AN-ti-*freez*) a substance that lowers the freezing point of a liquid

atmosphere (AT-muhss-fihr) the mixture of gases that surrounds Earth

carbon dioxide (KAR-buhn dye-OK-side) a greenhouse gas given off when fossil fuels are burned

clean (KLEEN) when something does not release harmful chemicals into the atmosphere

core (KOR) the center or innermost portion of Earth

crops (KROPS) plants that are grown and gathered, often for food

dye (DYE) to color or stain something

engineers (en-juh-NIHRZ) people who are trained to design and build machines

evaporate (i-VAP-uh-rayt) to dry up; to change from a liquid into a gas

fish farms (FISH FARMZ) places where fish are raised in tanks, mainly for food

fossil fuels (FOSS-uhl FYOO-uhlz) fuels such as coal, oil, and gas made from the remains of plants and animals that died millions of years ago

generators (JEN-uh-*ray*-turz) machines that produce electricity

geothermal (jee-oh-THUR-muhl) having to do with heat from inside Earth

geyser (GYE-zuhr) a spring that sprays hot water and steam into the air

global warming (GLOHB-uhl WORM-ing) the warming of Earth's air and oceans due to a buildup of greenhouse gases in Earth's atmosphere

greenhouses gases (GREEN-houss GASS-iz) carbon dioxide and other gases that trap warm air in Earth's atmosphere so it cannot escape into space

groundwater (GROUND-waw-tur) water found underground, trapped in soil or in cracks and holes in rocks

heat exchanger (HEET eks-CHAYNJ-ur) a system in which heat passes from one substance to another without the two substances mixing

hot springs (HOT SPRINGZ) sources of water that flow from the ground and are heated naturally within the earth

plant (PLANT) a factory

poisonous (POI-zuhn-uhss) able to kill or harm someone

pollute (puh-LOOT) release harmful substances into the air, water, or soil

power plants (POW-ur PLANTS) factories that produce electricity

renewable (re-NOO-uh-buhl) able to be replaced by a natural process in a short period of time

spas (SPAHZ) places where people go to relax by soaking in warm water that comes up from the earth

turbine (TUR-bine) an engine that is powered by wind, water, or steam moving through the blades of a wheel and making it spin

wells (WELZ) deep holes dug in the ground to get water

Index

Bibliography

Geothermal Education Office. http://geothermal.marin.org/

Montana Department of Commerce. http://commerce.mt.gov/energy/ geothermal/asp

U.S. Department of Energy. www.nrel.gov/docs/fy04osti/36316.pdf

Read More

Gleason, Carrie. *Geothermal Energy: Using Earth's Furnace (Energy Revolution).* New York: Crabtree Publishing Company (2008).

Orr, Tamra. *Geothermal Energy (Power Up!).* Ann Arbor, MI: Cherry Lake Publishing (2008).

Saunders, Nigel. *Geothermal Energy (Energy for the Future and Global Warming).* Pleasantville, NY: Gareth Stevens Publishing (2008).

Sherman, Josepha. *Geothermal Power.* Mankato, MN: Capstone Press (2004).

About the Author

Nancy White has written many science and nature books for children. She lives in New York's Hudson River Valley.